D0842916

SUPER QUARTERBACKS
12 GREAT LEADERS FROM NFL HISTORY

by Matt Tustison

12 STORY LIBRARY

www.12StoryLibrary.com

12-Story Library is an imprint of Peterson Publishing Company and Press Room Editions.

Produced for 12-Story Library by Red Line Editorial

Photographs ©: Charles Krupa/AP Images, cover, 1, 27; Pro Football Hall of Fame/AP Images, 4; Harris & Ewing/Library of Congress, 5; AP Images, 6, 9, 10, 12, 13; Al Messerschmidt/ AP Images, 14, 16, 28, 29; NFL Photos/AP Images, 17; Paul Spinelli/NFL Photos/AP Images, 19; Kevin Terrell/AP Images, 21; David Stluka/AP Images, 22; Doug Mills/AP Images, 23; Alex Brandon/AP Images, 24; Patric Schneider/AP Images, 25; Gene Lower/AP Images, 26

ISBN
978-1-63235-155-5 (hardcover)
978-1-63235-195-1 (paperback)
978-1-62143-247-0 (hosted ebook)

Library of Congress Control Number: 2015934300

Printed in the United States of America
Mankato, MN
June, 2015

Go beyond the book. Get free, up-to-date content on this topic at 12StoryLibrary.com.

TABLE OF CONTENTS

SAMMY BAUGH POPULARIZES THE FORWARD PASS

Sammy Baugh's nickname was "Slingin' Sammy." When Baugh was in high school in Texas, he tied a rope to a tire and hung it from a tree. He practiced throwing his football through the middle of the tire. He threw from 10 yards away, then moved out to 15 and 20 yards. He tried throwing while he ran. He did this for hours. He became very accurate.

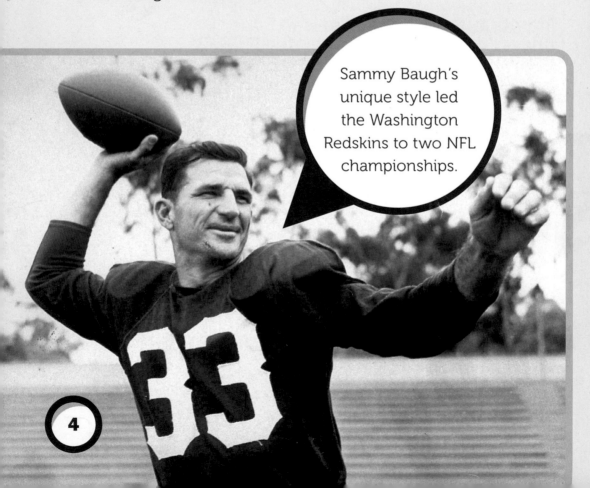

Sammy Baugh's unique style led the Washington Redskins to two NFL championships.

Baugh joined the Washington Redskins of the National Football League (NFL) in 1937. Before then, quarterbacks rarely passed the ball. Running plays were far more common. Baugh is known for making the forward pass a bigger part of pro football. He showed that passing forward was the fastest way to move the ball and score touchdowns.

When Baugh retired after the 1952 season, he held 13 NFL records. These included most passing yards and most touchdown passes. Baugh was a defensive back and a punter, too. He was famous as a triple threat. In 1943, Baugh led the NFL in pass completions, pass attempts, and completion percentage. The same season, he ranked first in punting average and led all defensive players with 11 interceptions.

Baugh guided the Redskins to NFL championships in 1937 and 1942. They also reached three more title games with Baugh calling the shots.

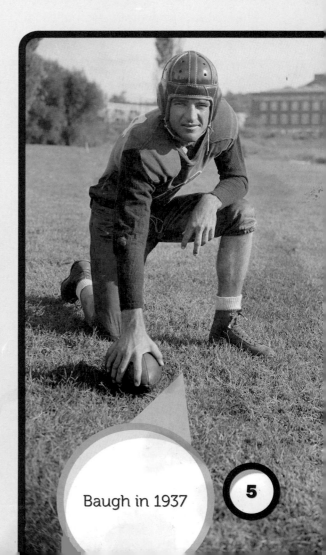

Baugh in 1937

6
Pro Bowls Sammy Baugh was selected for from 1938 to 1951.

- Baugh led NFL in passing yards four times (1937, 1940, 1947, 1948).
- Baugh led the NFL in punting average for four straight years (1940–43) and again in 1945.

OTTO GRAHAM LEADS BROWNS TO 10 TITLE GAMES

Otto Graham played just 10 years of pro football. Yet "Automatic Otto" led the Cleveland Browns to the league championship game in each of those 10 seasons. In all, Graham and the Browns won seven of those games.

Otto Graham drives through the offensive line for a touchdown. Graham's score helped the Cleveland Browns beat the Los Angeles Rams in the 1955 NFL title game.

.810

Career NFL winning percentage for Otto Graham. It was still the highest ever for a quarterback through the 2014 season.

- Graham had a career NFL record of 57–13–1.
- Graham made the Pro Bowl every year from 1950–54.

A MULTISPORT ATHLETE

Otto Graham was more than simply a great quarterback. In addition to pro football, he also played pro basketball. Graham played with the Rochester Royals during the 1945–46 season. He helped them win the National Basketball League title.

Graham played before the Super Bowl existed. He even played for the Browns before they joined the NFL. From 1946–49, he led Cleveland to the All America Football Conference title. The Browns joined the NFL after that. And they immediately captured that league's title, too. The Browns appeared in the next five NFL Championship Games, as well. They won it in 1954 and 1955.

Graham was the first pro quarterback to win 100 games. He averaged 9.0 yards per pass attempt over his career. This is still the best in NFL history.

After the 1954 season, Graham announced he was retiring from football at age 33. But the Browns struggled to find a quarterback in training camp in 1955. Their coach, Paul Brown, asked Graham to return to the team. Graham agreed, and the Browns won the title again. Graham ran for two touchdowns against the Los Angeles Rams in the championship game. Graham soon announced that he was retiring again. And this time he meant it.

JOHNNY UNITAS GUIDES COLTS TO "GREATEST GAME" WIN

Born in Pittsburgh, Johnny Unitas always wanted to play for the Steelers. He was excited when the hometown team drafted him in 1955. But the Steelers released the rookie quarterback before he had a chance to prove himself. So the skinny Unitas took a construction job that fall. He played for the Bloomfield Rams. They were a semipro team in Pittsburgh. In 1956, he was invited to try out for the NFL's Baltimore Colts. This time he made the team.

By 1958, Unitas had become stronger and grown into a star. He led Baltimore to the NFL title game against the New York Giants. The thrilling game was tied and went into overtime. The first team to score would win.

Unitas was known for calling daring plays. And that is what he did. Unitas had led the Colts to the Giants' 7-yard line. The Giants were expecting a running play. But Unitas passed to receiver Jim Mutscheller. On the next play, the Colts scored a touchdown on Alan Ameche's

47

Consecutive games, from 1956 to 1960, in which Johnny Unitas threw a touchdown pass. This was the NFL record for 52 years.

- The 1958 NFL Championship Game was the first to be broadcast on national TV.
- Unitas made the Pro Bowl 10 times between 1957 and 1967.

Baltimore Colts quarterback Johnny Unitas throws a pass against the Dallas Cowboys in 1969.

1-yard run. That gave Baltimore a 23–17 win.

Unitas threw for 349 yards and a touchdown that day. The game became known as "The Greatest Game Ever Played."

"Johnny U," as Unitas was called, stood out with his crew-cut hairstyle and his high-top cleats. He rarely had much to say to the media. But no one questioned his leadership. He was called a "field general."

Unitas finished his NFL career in 1973. He threw for 40,239 yards and 290 touchdowns. Both were league records at the time. Unitas helped the Colts win three NFL titles and a Super Bowl.

BART STARR HELPS GREEN BAY BECOME "TITLETOWN"

Bart Starr wasn't selected until the 17th round of the 1956 NFL Draft. And he didn't play very much at first. His team, the Green Bay Packers, weren't very good. So success came hard to Starr.

In 1959, Vince Lombardi was hired to coach the Packers. Lombardi liked Starr. He saw that Starr was smart and a leader. And before long, Green Bay was being called "Titletown, USA."

Green Bay Packers quarterback Bart Starr takes off running with the ball against the Detroit Lions in 1966.

"THE ICE BOWL"

The Packers trailed the Cowboys 17–14 late in the 1967 NFL title game. Bart Starr led Green Bay down the field. Then it was third down at Dallas' 1-yard line. Starr called the team's final timeout with 16 seconds left. Starr decided he could sneak the ball in. He tucked the ball into his belly and smashed his way in for a touchdown. Green Bay won 21–17.

Starr became the most-winning quarterback of his time. He helped guide the Packers to five championships, including two Super Bowl titles. He won Most Valuable Player (MVP) honors in Super Bowls I and II. But he might be most famous for his performance in the 1967 NFL Championship Game. The Packers beat the Dallas Cowboys in a game known as "The Ice Bowl." The temperature at Lambeau Field on that December day was -13˚F (-25˚C) at the start of the game.

Starr was at his best in his many playoff appearances. His Packers lost to the Philadelphia Eagles in the 1960 title game. After that, they never lost another postseason game under Starr, going 9–0.

294
Consecutive passes without an interception for Bart Starr from 1964 to 1965. This was an NFL record for 26 years.

- In 1961, Starr and the Packers beat the New York Giants for their first title in 17 years.
- Starr was named the NFL and Super Bowl MVP in the 1966 season.

THINK ABOUT IT

All of the quarterbacks in this book are over 6 feet tall. Why do you think it is important for a quarterback to be that tall?

ROGER STAUBACH TURNS INTO "CAPTAIN COMEBACK"

Roger Staubach graduated from the US Naval Academy in 1965. He had been drafted by the Dallas Cowboys the previous year. But he didn't play for the Cowboys until 1969. That is because he was committed to four years of service in the navy. He was 27 years old when he reported to the Cowboys.

Toward the end of the 1971 season, Staubach became the Cowboys' starting quarterback. He remained there through the 1970s.

Staubach was called "Roger the Dodger." This was because he liked to run with the ball while dodging the defense. He was also known

Dallas Cowboys quarterback Roger Staubach calls out the signals before a play in Super Bowl XII.

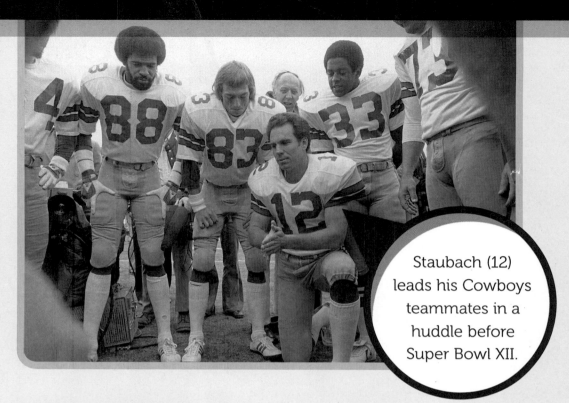

Staubach (12) leads his Cowboys teammates in a huddle before Super Bowl XII.

as "Captain Comeback." He earned this name for his 15 fourth-quarter, come-from-behind wins.

He posted an outstanding 85–29 record as a starter in his career. With a strong passing arm and scrambling skills, Staubach proved to be one of the most dangerous quarterbacks the league had ever seen.

Staubach led the Cowboys to two Super Bowl wins. They beat the Miami Dolphins in January 1972 and the Denver Broncos in January 1978. Through the 2014 season, he was one of just 11 quarterbacks with at least two Super Bowl victories as a starter.

4

Super Bowls the Cowboys played in with Roger Staubach as the starter. They won two.

- Staubach was the MVP of Super Bowl VI in January 1972.
- Staubach completed 12 of 19 passes for 119 yards and two touchdowns in Super Bowl VI.

13

TERRY BRADSHAW GOES 4-FOR-4 IN SUPER BOWLS

Pittsburgh Steelers quarterback Terry Bradshaw looks for an open receiver in Super Bowl XIII.

2

Seasons (1978 and 1982) in which Terry Bradshaw led the NFL in touchdown passes.

- Bradshaw won the NFL MVP Award in 1978.
- Today, we can watch Bradshaw on television during NFL broadcasts.

THINK ABOUT IT

Which of the 12 quarterbacks in this book would you rank the best of all time? Why? List at least three reasons that support your choice.

The Pittsburgh Steelers picked Terry Bradshaw first overall in the 1970 draft. The young quarterback had a strong arm. But his passes frequently were off-target. He threw 24 interceptions that season. That was the most in the NFL.

But by 1974, Bradshaw and the rest of the Steelers had blossomed. Pittsburgh had an amazing defense. It became known as the "Steel Curtain." The Steelers also had future Hall of Famers in running back Franco Harris and wide receivers Lynn Swann and John Stallworth. But Bradshaw was a key part of the team's success.

Bradshaw became the first quarterback to win four Super Bowls. Through the 2014 season, only Joe Montana and Tom Brady had matched that feat. The Steelers won Super Bowls following the 1974, 1975, 1978, and 1979 seasons. In those four Super Bowl victories, Bradshaw threw for a combined 932 yards and nine touchdowns. He was twice Super Bowl MVP.

CALLING HIS OWN PLAYS

As a rookie, Terry Bradshaw said he "never studied the game, never looked at films the way a quarterback should." However, Bradshaw learned to become a student of the game. He developed into a winning quarterback who called all his own plays.

JOE MONTANA STAYS COOL UNDER PRESSURE

Nothing seemed to faze Joe Montana. He was a master of the last-ditch drive. He led his teams to

San Francisco 49ers quarterback Joe Montana looks to pass in a 1986 game.

31 fourth-quarter comeback victories. His nickname became "Joe Cool."

When Montana was a kid, he almost quit his football team in Monongahela, Pennsylvania. But his father wouldn't let him. "Get your uniform," his dad said. "You're going back to practice."

The San Francisco 49ers should be thankful Montana kept playing football. He led his team to four Super Bowl titles in four tries. That run of success began with one famous drive.

The 49ers were playing the Dallas Cowboys on January 10, 1982. The winner would go to the Super Bowl. But Dallas led by six with time running out. Montana

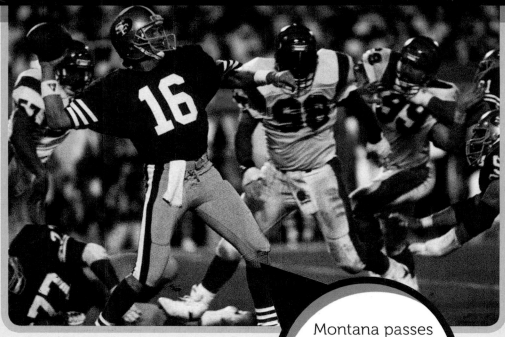

Montana passes against the Cincinnati Bengals in Super Bowl XXIII.

was ready. He led his team down the field. Finally, with 51 seconds left, he threw a pass into the end zone. Wide receiver Dwight Clark leaped high into the air to snatch the ball. "The Catch" led the 49ers to a 28–27 win. San Francisco went on to capture its first Super Bowl that year by beating the Cincinnati Bengals.

Seven years later, in Super Bowl XXIII, the 49ers were trailing the Bengals 16–13 with 3:10 remaining. Montana completed eight of nine passes on a 92-yard drive. With 34 seconds left, he hit John Taylor with a game-winning, 10-yard touchdown pass. San Francisco won again, 20–16.

11
Touchdown passes Joe Montana completed in four Super Bowl appearances. He threw no interceptions.

- Montana led the 49ers' pass-happy West Coast offense.
- Montana was Super Bowl MVP in three of his four appearances.

JOHN ELWAY CAPS CAREER WITH TWO SUPER BOWL TITLES

John Elway was tall and strong. He had big hands and long legs. And he never gave up. Elway's father was his college football coach. He taught Elway and encouraged him.

Elway took the Denver Broncos to five Super Bowls. Some people criticized him when the Broncos lost the first three. Elway replied, "How many guys never even got there?"

Then, in Elway's last two seasons, he took the next step. In January 1998, he led the Broncos to a 31–24 win over the Green Bay Packers in Super Bowl XXXII. One year later, he led Denver to a 34–19 win over the Atlanta Falcons in Super Bowl XXXIII. Elway made his last game a memorable one. He threw for 336 yards and a touchdown. Plus he ran for another touchdown. Elway was named the game's MVP.

THINK ABOUT IT

The first three times John Elway made it to the Super Bowl, his team lost. Some people considered that to be failure. What do you think? Is getting to the Super Bowl a great accomplishment, even if your team loses?

7

Consecutive seasons in which John Elway passed for at least 3,000 yards and rushed for at least 200 yards. That is an NFL record.

- Elway rushed for 3,407 yards in his career. That ranks seventh all-time for a quarterback.
- Elway was the NFL MVP in 1987.

John Elway celebrates after leading the Denver Broncos to victory in Super Bowl XXXII.

"THE DRIVE"

The Broncos played the Cleveland Browns on January 11, 1987. The winner would go to the Super Bowl. John Elway led the Broncos on what has become known as "The Drive." The 98-yard, 15-play march down the field in the final minutes of regulation forced overtime. Elway threw a 5-yard pass to Mark Jackson for the tying touchdown. Denver went on to beat the Browns 23–20 in overtime.

DAN MARINO SMASHES PASSING RECORDS

Dan Marino joined the Miami Dolphins in 1983. He led the team to the Super Bowl after the 1984 season. But the Dolphins lost 38–16 to Joe Montana and the San Francisco 49ers. Marino never did return to the Super Bowl. But he made his mark on NFL history with his passing statistics.

Marino had one of the most brilliant seasons in NFL history in 1984. He passed for 5,084 yards and 48 touchdowns. That shattered both records. The previous record for touchdown passes was 36. The record for passing yards had been 4,802. Marino's records have since been broken. But he set his records in an era where quarterbacks didn't pass as often.

"This boy is in a class by himself," said former New York Giants

quarterback Y. A. Tittle, who had shared the old touchdown record. "There is just no denying that."

Marino retired following the 1999 season. It was his 17th year in the NFL, all with the Dolphins. He was the all-time leader in touchdown throws (420) and passing yardage (61,361) at that point. Marino was slow-footed. But because of his passing skills, he was sacked less often than most quarterbacks.

13
Times Dan Marino passed for 400 or more yards in a game. Only Peyton Manning has done so more times.

- Marino was the 1984 NFL MVP.
- Marino was named to nine Pro Bowls from 1983 to 1995.

Miami Dolphins quarterback Dan Marino passes against the Washington Redskins in a 1984 game.

10

BRETT FAVRE BRINGS A TITLE BACK TO GREEN BAY

Brett Favre played wide receiver as a fifth grader growing up in Mississippi. Then, one day, he fell on the ball. It knocked the wind out of him. That was it. He had enough of playing receiver.

"I want to play quarterback," Favre told his coach.

Favre took over as quarterback, threw for a touchdown, and ran for two more that day. He had found his position. When Favre became a starting quarterback with the Green Bay Packers in 1992, he was a fiery leader. But he was a wild passer. Packers coach Mike Holmgren was

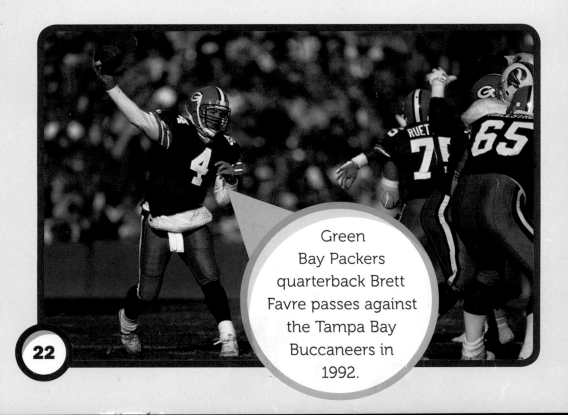

Green Bay Packers quarterback Brett Favre passes against the Tampa Bay Buccaneers in 1992.

297

Consecutive games started by Brett Favre from 1992 to 2010. This is the most by any position player in NFL history.

- The Atlanta Falcons drafted Favre but traded him to the Packers after one season.
- Favre was the NFL MVP in 1995, 1996, and 1997.

ENDING WITH THE ENEMY

After 16 seasons with the Packers, Brett Favre was beloved in Green Bay. But the Packers were ready to move on before he was. So Favre played the 2008 season with the New York Jets. Then he joined the Minnesota Vikings, one of the Packers' main rivals. He even led the Vikings to the conference championship game in 2009.

patient. It paid off. Favre learned to play more under control.

In January 1997, Favre and Green Bay beat the New England Patriots 35–21 in Super Bowl XXXI. Favre threw for two touchdowns. It was the Packers' first NFL crown since 1967. "Titletown, USA" finally had another championship.

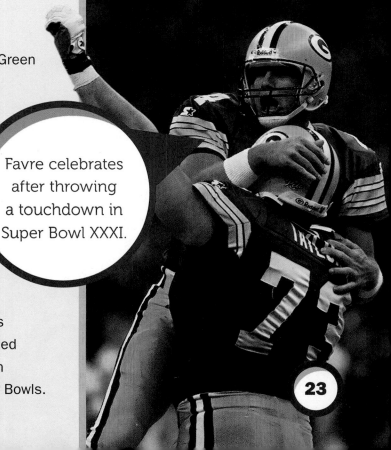

Favre celebrates after throwing a touchdown in Super Bowl XXXI.

In 16 seasons as the team's starting quarterback, Favre led Green Bay to 11 postseason appearances and two Super Bowls.

PEYTON MANNING MAKES AMAZING COMEBACK

Peyton Manning has received many honors. But one award that he is especially proud of is the 2012 NFL Comeback Player of the Year.

Before Manning had to come back, he was one of the game's biggest stars. The Indianapolis Colts drafted Manning first overall in 1998. He quickly developed into the game's best passer. In 2004, Manning threw for a record-breaking 49 touchdowns. Then in the playoffs

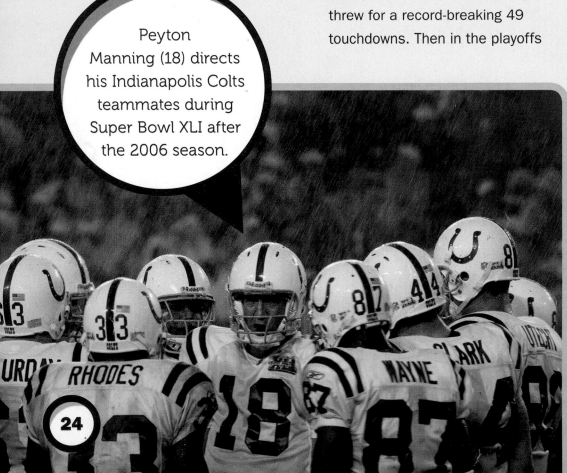

Peyton Manning (18) directs his Indianapolis Colts teammates during Super Bowl XLI after the 2006 season.

after the 2006 season, he guided the Colts to the Super Bowl. Indianapolis beat the Chicago Bears. Manning was the Super Bowl MVP.

But in 2011, he needed to have neck surgery twice and sat out the entire season. The Colts released Manning before the 2012 season. Some doubted he could recover from the surgeries. But Denver believed in him. The Broncos signed Manning. He responded by passing for 37 touchdowns and leading the team to a 13–3 record in 2012.

"I feel very, very privileged," Manning said after accepting the comeback award. "I've certainly missed . . . playing the game that I love."

In 2013, Manning passed for 55 touchdowns and 5,477 yards. Those were both NFL single-season records. Manning and the Broncos made it to the Super Bowl in February 2014. But they fell to the Seattle Seahawks.

509

Touchdown passes Peyton Manning had thrown after he connected with Demaryius Thomas on October 19, 2014. This broke Brett Favre's NFL record.

- Manning was the NFL MVP in 2003, 2004, 2008, 2009, and 2013.
- In his first three years with the Broncos, Manning won 38 games and lost just 10.

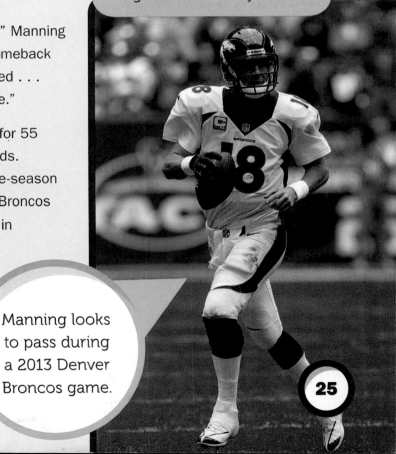

Manning looks to pass during a 2013 Denver Broncos game.

TOM BRADY FILLS IN AND GOES ON TO GREATNESS

There was a time when no one knew whether Tom Brady would even make it in the NFL. Brady wasn't selected until the sixth round of the 2000 NFL Draft. The New England Patriots selected him. But he played in only one game as a rookie. That changed early in the 2001 season. The Patriots' starter was injured in the second game. Brady started the next week. He has been the starter ever since.

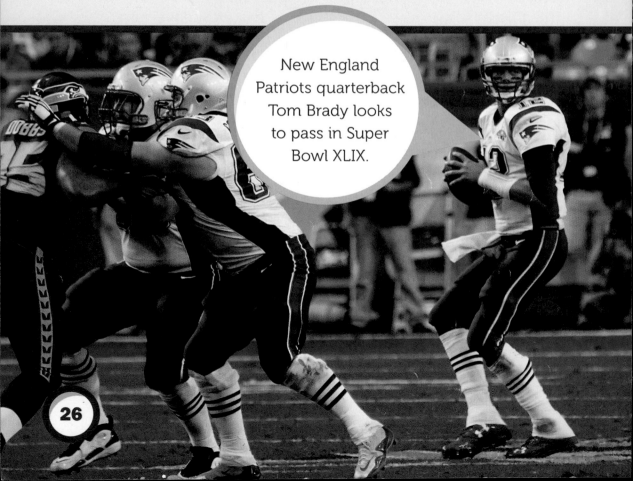

New England Patriots quarterback Tom Brady looks to pass in Super Bowl XLIX.

Brady learned quickly. Remarkably, he guided New England to the Super Bowl that season. The Patriots were big underdogs against the St. Louis Rams. With 1:21 left and the game tied, New England had the ball but no timeouts. No matter. Brady coolly led the Patriots down the field. He spiked the ball to stop the clock with seven seconds left. Adam Vinatieri came on and made a 48-yard field goal. The Patriots won 20–17. Brady, just 24 years old, was the game's MVP. "It's just an overwhelming feeling," he said.

Led by Brady, the Patriots went on to five more Super Bowls through the 2014 season. They won back-to-back titles after the 2003 and 2004 seasons. Then they added another title after the 2014 season.

Brady, called "Tom Terrific" by some, has established himself as an all-time great.

3

Number of Super Bowl MVP Awards for Tom Brady.

- Brady's two Super Bowl losses came in upsets against the New York Giants.
- Only Brady and Joe Montana have won multiple regular-season and Super Bowl MVP awards.

A WINNER WHEN IT MATTERS

Through the 2014 season, Tom Brady had a 21–8 playoff record. The 21 wins are the most by a quarterback in NFL history.

FUN FACTS AND STORIES

- When Redskins star Sammy Baugh wasn't playing football, he competed in rodeos. His specialty was calf roping. He threw the rope the same way he threw the football.

- One of Roger Staubach's career highlights came in a 1975 playoff game at Minnesota. The Cowboys trailed the Vikings 14–10, and only 32 seconds remained. Staubach unloaded a long pass from midfield to receiver Drew Pearson. The pass was underthrown. There was contact, and Vikings defensive back Nate Wright fell to the turf. Pearson caught the ball and ran into the end zone. The Vikings pleaded that pass interference should have been called. But the referees disagreed. The Cowboys won 17–14 on Staubach's "Hail Mary" pass.

- Brett Favre showed a strong arm early in life. One of Favre's teachers recalled the youngster throwing 50-yard passes in the fifth grade. Irv Favre, Brett's father, said that starting around the fifth grade, Brett had "a fire in his eyes that never went away."

- After the Colts won the 1958 NFL Championship Game, Johnny Unitas turned down $750 in fees for TV appearances scheduled for that night and the following morning. He did this so he could be with the team on the trip back to Baltimore.

- Joe Montana was known for his ability to stay calm under pressure. But even his San Francisco 49ers' teammates were surprised in Super Bowl XXIII after the 1988 season. With the 49ers trailing the Cincinnati Bengals 16–13 and just over three minutes left, Montana stepped into the huddle. "Isn't that John Candy?" he said, pointing to the famous comedian in the stands. Montana then proceeded to lead his team on the game-winning drive.

GLOSSARY

accurate
Free from mistakes or errors.

daring
Bold or courageous. Fearless or adventurous.

draft
An event held each year in which NFL teams select players who are new to the league.

Pro Bowl
The NFL all-star game.

retire
To end one's football career, usually because of age.

rival
An opponent that brings out great emotion in a team and its fans.

rookie
A first-year player.

sack
When a defensive player tackles the offense's quarterback before he can throw a pass.

scrambling
When a quarterback runs with the ball, often to avoid pressure from the defense.

semipro
Playing football for pay but on a part-time basis.

FOR MORE INFORMATION

Books

Editors of Sports Illustrated. *Sports Illustrated NFL QB: The Greatest Position in Sports.* New York: Sports Illustrated, 2014.

Editors of Sports Illustrated Kids. *Sports Illustrated Kids 1st and 10: Top 10 Lists of Everything in Football.* New York: Sports Illustrated Kids, 2011.

Garner, Joe, and Bob Costas. *100 Yards of Glory: The Greatest Moments in NFL History.* Boston: Houghton Mifflin Harcourt, 2011.

Websites

ESPN
www.espn.com

Monday Morning Quarterback
mmqb.si.com

National Football League
www.nfl.com

Pro Football Reference
www.pro-football-reference.com

INDEX

About the Author

Matt Tustison is a sports copyeditor at the *Washington Post*. He has also worked as a sports copyeditor at other newspapers including the *St. Paul Pioneer Press* and as an editor and writer of children's sports books at Red Line Editorial in Burnsville, Minnesota.

READ MORE FROM 12-STORY LIBRARY

Every 12-Story Library book is available in many formats, including Amazon Kindle and Apple iBooks. For more information, visit your device's store or 12StoryLibrary.com.